TECH PIONEERS™

ALAN TURING

REBECCA KRAFT RECTOR

ROSEN
PUBLISHING

NEW YORK

Published in 2016 by The Rosen Publishing Group, Inc.
29 East 21st Street, New York, NY 10010

Copyright © 2016 by The Rosen Publishing Group, Inc.

First Edition

Library of Congress Cataloging-in-Publication Data

Rector, Rebecca Kraft, author.
  Alan Turing / Rebecca Kraft Rector. — First Edition.
     pages cm. — (Tech pioneers)
  Includes bibliographical references and index.
  ISBN 978-1-4994-6280-7 (library bound)
  1. Turing, Alan Mathison, 1912–1954—Juvenile literature. 2. Mathematicians—Great Britain—Biography—Juvenile literature. 3. Computer scientists—Great Britain—Biography—Juvenile literature. I. Title.
  QA29.T8R43 2015
  510.92—dc23
  [B]
                                                            2015033176

Manufactured in China

CONTENTS

INTRODUCTION

Alan Mathison Turing was a British mathematician, logician, cryptographer, and computer science pioneer. He is considered by some to be the founder of computer science. His papers on artificial intelligence were groundbreaking. He also contributed greatly to research in the concept of artificial life.

Even as a child Alan had a curious mind, inventing words and "helpful" items like green paint for the stairs. His interest in mathematics and science worried the teachers at the private schools—known, confusingly, as public schools in Britain—that he attended. At that time, education focused on the classics and literature, and Alan typically got failing grades in those classes. He was also untidy in his clothing and sloppy in his homework. He often jumped to the correct answer without demonstrating that he knew how he got there. His teachers could not decide if Alan was a genius because of his grasp of advanced mathematics or a failure because of his lack of interest in literature.

Turing attended Cambridge University, in Cambridge, England, and received his Ph.D. from Princeton University in Princeton, New Jersey. One of his most

Alan Turing was not only a genius in computer science but also a code-breaking hero during World War II.

famous and influential papers was published at that time. In it, he set forth the idea of a Universal Turing Machine, a machine that could solve mathematical problems and perform other tasks for which it was given instructions. This idea is commonplace now but was novel and groundbreaking then. It laid the foundation for computer science.

When Britain entered World War II, Turing worked at the secret British code-breaking headquarters called Bletchley Park. The people working there were trying to decipher the coded messages that Germany was using to communicate with its army, air force, and naval forces. The code was called the Enigma code, and Turing built a device called the Bombe to break it. The Bombe was an innovative machine that enabled the British to crack the Enigma code and read German army and air force messages. Turing was also instrumental in breaking the more sophisticated Naval Enigma code.

Turing's code-breaking work remained top secret until the 1970s. Even after the war, Turing's family and friends did not know about the important contributions that he had made to the war effort. However, Great Britain's prime minister, Winston Churchill, was well aware of Turing's brilliant work. He said that the work at Bletchley Park might have shortened the war by as much as five years.

In 1950 Turing published another important paper. In it he proposed the Turing Test—a method to test a computer's intelligence. The Turing Test is a benchmark in artificial intelligence. Turing also contributed groundbreaking work in the field of artificial life.

A gay man at a time when it was a crime, Turing was arrested, tried, convicted, and punished. His death of cyanide poisoning at the age of forty-two was ruled a suicide. Later the British government apologized for his punishment and the queen issued an official pardon for his conviction.

Chapter One

BOY GENIUS AND BAD STUDENT

Alan Mathison Turing was born June 23, 1912, in London, England. His parents were Julius and Ethel Sara Turing. Although Alan was born in England, his father worked in India for the British government. He was in the Indian Civil Service. Alan's parents lived in India most of the time. Alan and his brother, John, who was four years older, lived in England and rarely saw their parents.

EARLY LIFE

While their parents served in India, Alan and his brother stayed in England with Colonel and Mrs. Ward and their four daughters. Other boys sometimes boarded with the family, too. Alan and John called Mrs. Ward "Granny

This map of the British Empire, with British colonies in red, shows the enormous distance between young Alan in Britain and his parents in India.

Ward." Their nanny was called "Nanny Thompson." Alan became friends with the older daughter, Hazel, and later in life he gave Hazel money so that she could become a missionary.

Alan did not fit in well with the Wards. Mrs. Ward complained that he was a bookworm. His mother scolded him in her letters for this.

As a young child Alan liked to make up words. A candle that was about to go out was a "greasicle." The noise of seagulls was "quockling." His mother recorded

ALAN TURING'S WORLD

Alan Turing was part of the upper middle class in Britain. His parents paid for him to go to exclusive, boys-only schools, though he sometimes received a scholarship. Children of the working class went to state schools.

The British Empire had colonies around the world. British citizens were sent to the colonies to help rule them. Alan's father was part of the group ruling India, called the Indian Civil Service. It was not unusual for British citizens who worked in other parts of the British Empire to leave their children in England to be raised by nannies and educated in boarding schools.

Alan's parents traveled by ship to India. The trip could take weeks, so they did not visit easily back and forth with their children. Airplanes were used during World War I, which started two years after Alan was born. But it was not until later that passenger air travel became common. The Wright brothers had flown their first airplane only nine years before Alan was born.

The Turing parents could not call their children on the phone. Homes were becoming connected by telephones and electricity, but telephone calls could not be placed across an ocean until 1927. Those calls were between New York and London. Families like the Turings stayed in touch by writing letters.

Radio technology was still fairly new and home television broadcasts were still decades away. And of course, computers had to wait for Alan Turing to grow up before they became a reality!

many of the words that he made up. He taught himself to read before he started school.

Even as a toddler he liked to experiment. When he was three he planted the broken arms and legs of a wooden sailor in the garden, sure that they would grow. When he was older he invented a powder to turn the steps green. He figured out how to extract iodine from seaweed. He made his own ink and fountain pen, along with many other items. Alan was interested in everything and everyone. People he met thought he was a charming child.

In the summer of 1918, Alan was sent to a day school called St. Michael's, in East Sussex, England. There his teachers complained of his untidiness. However, when he left the school at age nine, the headmistress said, "I have clever boys and hard-working boys, but Alan has genius." She mentioned how talented he was with numbers.

As Alan grew older he read books about nature and liked to study maps. When his mother returned from

India to visit, she found Alan changed. He was no longer outgoing and interested in other people. So, during 1921, his mother spent some time homeschooling him.

After a few months, he started at his brother's school, Hazelhurst. It was also in East Sussex. John was at the top of the school and Alan was at the bottom. It was at Hazelhurst that Alan first became interested in chess. He also continued to make his own inventions while he was there.

In 1922 Alan was given the book *Natural Wonders Every Child Should Know*. It was written by Edwin Tenney Brewster and featured illustrations showing how plants and animals grow and develop. Alan Turing spoke highly of this book, even when he was an adult.

Alan's schoolwork continued to be untidy and his handwriting was poor. He stuttered when answering questions. He continued to do well in subjects like math and when he was twelve and a half he began learning organic chemistry from an encyclopedia.

His father retired in 1926 and Alan's parents moved to the north of France. The boys continued to attend boarding school in England and visited their parents during the holidays.

SHERBORNE SCHOOL

At the age of thirteen, Alan won a place at the highly competitive Sherborne School in Dorset, England. By the

Alan probably learned how chicks hatch from one of his favorite books, *Natural Wonders Every Child Should Know*.

time school started, he was fourteen years old. Despite his young age, Alan planned to travel on his own from France—where he was staying with his parents during his vacation—to his new school. He took a boat from France but when he landed, he discovered that there was a transportation strike! He had no way to get to school sixty miles (96 kilometers) away. He sent a telegram to his new headmaster to say he would be there on time.

Then he set off on his bicycle, with a map. Alan stopped overnight at a hotel before arriving on time the next day. People were astonished that he had traveled such a long distance on his own. Even his headmaster admired his independence and determination. His feat was reported in the local paper.

Alan was still a poor student, untidy, inattentive, and jumping ahead in his books. He stammered when answering questions, and he couldn't keep his shirttail tucked in. His mother saved his school reports. They showed a mix of successes and failures. At age fifteen, he figured out an advanced mathematical formula on his own. He did not know someone else had already done it. His teachers described him as a "keen and able mathematician."

Alan won mathematics prizes but often failed his exams because he did not show how he reached his conclusions. His housemaster—the member of the school

Alan attended Sherborne School, a private boarding school next to Sherborne Abbey in Dorset, England.

staff who was in charge of the house where he lived—said Alan was "trying to build a roof before he had laid the foundations." One of his teachers said, "He spends a great deal of time in investigations in advanced mathematics to the neglect of his elementary work." Another teacher complained, "His work is so ill-presented that he ought to be sent down." However, yet another teacher said, "The boy is a genius and ought to be sent up." He was left where he was.

Elite education at this time focused on the classics and literature, which Alan did not excel in. Math and science were not as important to the schools and teachers. Alan's headmaster at Sherborne was concerned about Alan's interest in math and science, saying to his mother, "If he is to be solely a Scientific Specialist, he is wasting his time at a Public School." But his mother was determined that he stay at Sherborne and be educated like others of his class.

Alan had few friends. He enjoyed long-distance running, which could be done alone. He started running competitively and won races for his school. Alan finally found a friend in Christopher Morcom, who was a year older and a year ahead in school. Both boys were interested in math and science and enjoyed inventing their own codes. They performed experiments, discussed Einstein's theories, and studied the skies through a telescope. But on February 6, 1930, Christopher was rushed to the

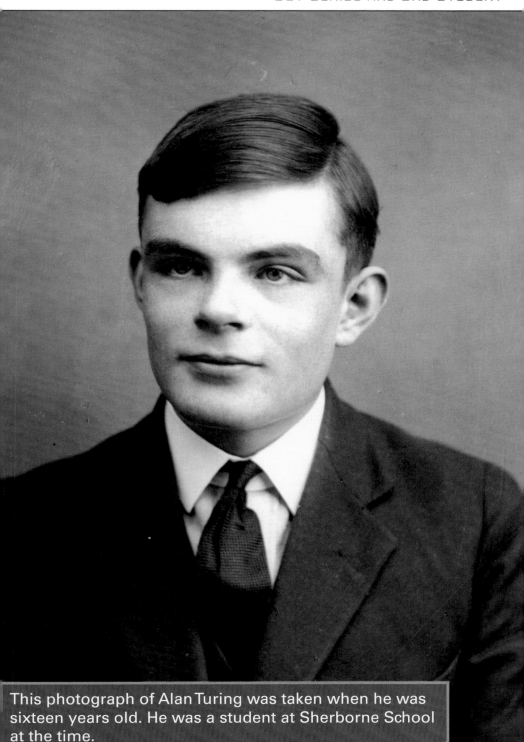

This photograph of Alan Turing was taken when he was sixteen years old. He was a student at Sherborne School at the time.

hospital. He died a week later of bovine tuberculosis. Bovine tuberculosis is a disease that is most often caused by drinking contaminated cow's milk or eating contaminated cheese as a child.

Alan was disconsolate. According to letters to his mother, he now felt he must do the work that he and Christopher were meant to do together and not let him down. Alan wrote a paper called "Nature of Spirit" to explain to Christopher's mother his thoughts about how the spirit "finds a new body sooner or later, perhaps immediately."

When the time came for him to leave Sherborne, Alan's teachers were still not satisfied with his work. One of them noted, "He thinks very rapidly and is apt to be 'brilliant' but unsound in some of his work. He is seldom defeated by a problem, but his methods are often crude, cumbersome and untidy." He was doing so poorly in his English and Latin classes that those teachers thought he should not even be allowed to take the exam that would allow him to graduate. However, he took the exam and passed.

KING'S COLLEGE AND PRINCETON

In December 1930 Alan took the Cambridge entrance exam, hoping to get a scholarship to Trinity College. He did not. However, King's College, also part of Cambridge, offered him a scholarship. King's College excelled in mathematics and science. His classmates recall Turing was shy and awkward, and he still stammered when he was excited. Turing joined the rowing club. He continued long-distance running, which he continued to win races in, too. He finished his degree in 1934. The following year, he was elected a Fellow of King's College. Fellows at Cambridge get funding to continue their studies. They are also part of the governing body of their colleges.

In 1936, one of Turing's most famous papers was published. It was called "On Computable Numbers, with an Application to the Entscheidungsproblem." In an interview with the London *Times*, Turing's nephew, Sir John Dermot Turing—who is also a mathematician—said that his uncle showed "there would always be propositions that could neither be proved true or false." In order to prove this concept, Alan Turing imagined the Universal Turing Machine. As his nephew explained, it "could imitate other machines—and you could program it to do what you liked. This was considered to be the foundation paper for computer science."

That same year, Turing headed for the United States to study mathematical logic at Princeton University. While there, he studied codes and ciphers. Codes and ciphers (which British spell "cyphers") are ways to keep information secret. They are frequently used to conceal important information from an enemy. A coded

TRANSPOSITION AND SUBSTITUTION CIPHERS

There are several kinds of ciphers. In a transposition cipher, the letters of words are simply rearranged, or transposed. The original letters do not change. Changing "SUBMARINE" to "NAMBRUESI" is a simple transposition cipher. All of the letters in "SUBMARINE" are still there, simply in a different place.

Another variety of transposition cipher can be made by placing the plaintext letters in order on a grid. The message is encoded by taking the letters from the grid in a different order. The letters may be taken top to bottom, bottom to top, or side to side.

In addition to transposition, ciphers can also be created using substitution. Each letter remains in its original position. However, it is replaced by a different letter or symbol. There are many substitution ciphers, and experts use complex versions. A simple substitution cipher would be to replace each letter with the one that follows it alphabetically. For example, "ENEMY" would become "FOFNZ."

A more complicated form of a substitution cipher would be to replace the letters. The new letters would then be broken into blocks that are the same length. This hides the word breaks. If you used the simple cipher described above, "ENEMY SIGHTED AHEAD" becomes "FO FN ZT JH IU FE BI FBE."

or enciphered message can be sent openly. The meaning of the message is hidden, not the message itself. People have used codes and ciphers for thousands of years. For example, the Roman general Julius Caesar is known to have sent his generals important information concealed with a cipher. Experts can create extremely complicated codes and ciphers.

The word "code" is often used to mean both a code and a cipher. But there is a difference between a code and a cipher. Technically, in a code, an entire word is replaced by another word. Symbols or numbers could also replace the word. Codes are difficult to memorize, so a key or codebook is used. The codebook will list words in normal language (called plaintext) and what code words to use to replace them. If a ship or army is about to be captured, it is essential to destroy the codebook. If the enemy captures the codebook, then it will be able to read all messages, even important communications between commanders.

```
  A B C D E F G H I J K L M N O P Q R S T U V W X Y

A A B C D E F G H I J K L M N O P Q R S T U V W X Y
B B C D E F G H I J K L M N O P Q R S T U V W X Y Z
C C D E F G H I J K L M N O P Q R S T U V W X Y Z A
D D E F G H I J K L M N O P Q R S T U V W X Y Z A B
E E F G H I J K L M N O P Q R S T U V W X Y Z A B C
F F G H I J K L M N O P Q R S T U V W X Y Z A B C D
G G H I J K L M N O P Q R S T U V W X Y Z A B C D E
H H I J K L M N O P Q R S T U V W X Y Z A B C D E F
I I J K L M N O P Q R S T U V W X Y Z A B C D E F G
J J K L M N O P Q R S T U V W X Y Z A B C D E F G H
K K L M N O P Q R S T U V W X Y Z A B C D E F G H I
L L M N O P Q R S T U V W X Y Z A B C D E F G H I J
M M N O P Q R S T U V W X Y Z A B C D E F G H I J K
N N O P Q R S T U V W X Y Z A B C D E F G H I J K L
O O P Q R S T U V W X Y Z A B C D E F G H I J K L M
P P Q R S T U V W X Y Z A B C D E F G H I J K L M N
Q Q R S T U V W X Y Z A B C D E F G H I J K L M N O
R R S T U V W X Y Z A B C D E F G H I J K L M N O P
S S T U V W X Y Z A B C D E F G H I J K L M N O P Q
T T U V W X Y Z A B C D E F G H I J K L M N O P Q R
U U V W X Y Z A B C D E F G H I J K L M N O P Q R S
V V W X Y Z A B C D E F G H I J K L M N O P Q R S T
W W X Y Z A B C D E F G H I J K L M N O P Q R S T U
X X Y Z A B C D E F G H I J K L M N O P Q R S T U V
Y Y Z A B C D E F G H I J K L M N O P Q R S T U V W
Z Z A B C D E F G H I J K L M N O P Q R S T U V W X
```

cipher	VVVRBACP
key	COVERCOVER...
plaintext	THANKYOU

The letters THA from THANKYOU intersect with the letters COV from COVERCOVER at V, V, and V to provide the first letters of this cipher.

A cipher is a method of concealing written information by replacing one letter with another letter. A number or symbol can also replace the letter.

Without a codebook or a key, it can be difficult to break a code or cipher. During wartime, governments have people specially trained in code breaking. The procedure of code breaking is called cryptanalysis.

Turing made up his own codes and designed a cipher machine. He was proud of one of his codes, saying that it was fast to encode and practically impossible to break. Turing received his Ph.D. in 1938 and was offered a job at Princeton. Instead, he decided to return to Cambridge.

Chapter Two

Ultra Versus Enigma

I n 1938, Turing returned to King's College, Cambridge, and secretly began working part-time for the British Code and Cypher School at an old mansion called Bletchley Park, in Buckinghamshire, England.

In August 1939, Germany invaded Poland. Great Britain had signed a treaty to assist Poland, but Hitler, Germany's leader, was determined to invade anyway. Three days later both Great Britain and France declared war on Germany. Soon, Australia, Canada, New Zealand, and South Africa joined the war. World War II had begun.

The day after Britain declared war, Turing moved to an inn near Bletchley Park and went to work full-time. He bicycled to work—three miles (5 km) each way. His family thought he was a civil servant in the Department of Communications.

In reality, Turing joined a team of mathematicians, language specialists, chess masters, and experts at solving crossword puzzles. Their mission was to break the radio code that Germany was using for its military messages. The code was called Enigma, and it was produced on a machine that resembled an old-fashioned typewriter. Germany sent thousands of coded messages a day—some important, some merely weather reports. Those fighting against the Germans (called the Allies) intercepted these messages and tried to decode them. The information gathered from these messages was called Ultra and the task of breaking the code was Project Ultra.

BUILDING THE BOMBE

Before Britain entered the war, mathematicians in the Polish Cipher Bureau had figured out the Enigma code and decoded German messages from 1933 to 1939 using a machine they called *Bomba*. They gave Britain and France all their information when Britain entered the war in September 1939. However, in May 1940, the Germans changed their methods. The Enigma code was once again very difficult to break.

British agents captured two German Enigma machines and gave them to the teams at Bletchley Park. This helped everyone understand how the machines worked. Not only did the machines demonstrate how the

German messages were put into code but they could also decode the messages. But first Turing and the others had to figure out—for each message—the starting points of the Enigma machine's three wheels.

The wheels changed letters into code. The position of the wheels constantly changed, but if the starting position could be determined, the code could be broken. This

Bletchley Park was the top-secret location of the British Code and Cypher School during World War II. The work there remained secret until the 1970s.

was a difficult task, though, since there were billions of possible settings.

One thing that helped the code breakers throughout the war was a crib. The word "crib" often means a cheat sheet or list of answers to a test. To the code breakers, it meant a word or phrase in German that often showed up in messages. Since the messages were often sent in several parts,

one phrase that appeared often was "continuation of previous message." This long German phrase was abbreviated to "FORT," and the code breakers were often successful in finding it. Since many messages were weather reports, the German abbreviation for weather station, "WEWA," was another popular crib. Others were "EINS," which means "one," and "FEIND," which means "enemy." The German phrases for "weather for the night" and "beacons lit as ordered" also came up frequently.

THE ENIGMA MACHINE

The Enigma code was produced on a machine that had three letter wheels that could be set at various starting points. The Enigma machine was the size and shape of an old-fashioned typewriter with letter keys. But it also had another set of letters above the first set. This second set of letters would light up as the message was typed. The machine was battery-powered, and there was a lightbulb under each letter. An assistant watched for the lit letters and wrote them down. This was the coded message that was then transmitted by Morse code, often by a third person. Three people would also be required to decode the message.

Within one message each letter would not always be coded in the same way. In other words, B might be coded as W at one point, and M at another. This was because the wheels rotated as the letters were typed. There were also wires that could be plugged into different places. There were billions of possible settings. This made the Enigma code very difficult to break.

Polish mathematician Marian Rejewski figured out a method to discover the starting position of the wheels that had been used to encode a message. Once the Poles knew this, they built a machine to decode the messages. They called their deciphering machine *Bomba*. From 1933

(continued on page 30)

The Enigma machine's three wheels are above the lighted letter board. Below the letter board are the keyboard and plugboard.

(continued from page 28)

to 1939 the Polish decoded German messages. After Germans changed their methods, though, the starting position of the wheels could no longer be determined using Rejewski's method.

The reason cribs could work with Enigma was that the Enigma machine never encoded a letter as itself. So an "M" could never be "M" in an Enigma message. When using a crib, this ruled out many possibilities. The code breaker could compare the crib to the message by sliding it over the coded letters. If any of the letters matched, then that was the wrong position for the crib. If there was a match, the

crib was said to "crash." With a long crib, it sometimes ruled out every position except the correct one. However, if the crib was not in the coded message, it crashed completely. Even with cribs, decoding Enigma was difficult and slow. The team at Bletchley Park needed a breakthrough.

Turing knew that a machine could check the possible settings much more quickly than the team of code breakers could. He improved the Polish *Bomba* until he had developed the more powerful Bombe. Another Cambridge mathematician, W. G. Welchman, also made important contributions to the British machine. The

This is the front panel of a Bombe, showing the drums that worked in the same way that the Enigma wheels did.

Bombe searched the various combinations of the Enigma machine's wheels at a speed much faster than a human. It searched for the connections that would decode the message back into German.

The Bombe was a success. The original Bombe was used from 1940 through late 1941, when a new version of it was introduced. At that point the team at Bletchley had fifteen Bombes working to break codes used by the German Luftwaffe (air force) and army.

The Bombe was over seven feet (2.1 meters) long and taller than a person. It had ten miles (16 km) of wire in it. It was not a single machine. It was actually thirty reproduction Enigma machines joined together. The way the machines were joined could be changed according to how the code breakers wanted to work on a message. Eventually the machines worked all day and all night, tended by members of the Women's Royal Navy Service (who were known as Wrens). By the end of the war, there were about two hundred Bombes and two thousand Wrens working at Bletchley. The women were doing top-secret work so they were never allowed to be assigned anywhere else in case information was leaked.

THE PROF

The women at Bletchley Park described most of the men there as "weird." Even among the other weird men, Tur-

About 75 percent of the people who worked at Bletchley Park during World War II were women. They included the Wrens seen here.

ing stood out. He was tall, with dark hair and deep-set blue eyes.

He was known as "the Prof." When his mother called there, no one knew who Mr. Turing was because most people knew him only as the Prof! Turing wore shabby clothes, sometimes used a necktie or a piece of string for a belt, and put on his gas mask to bicycle to work. He had a practical reason for wearing the gas mask. He suffered from hay fever and the gas mask stopped him from breathing in pollen. It may have been practical, but it was different. Turing also did not look at people. He picked at his fingernails, and he went sideways through doors. The Prof could be solitary and did not do things in the usual way.

Turing continued to distress his superiors as he had done with his teachers. One complained in a letter, "Turing is very difficult to anchor down. He is very clever but quite irresponsible."

Turing joined the Home Guard so he could learn how to handle a rifle in case Britain was invaded. But he stopped attending the gatherings after he became an excellent shot. When he was brought up for court martial—or trial in a military court—he told them to check his application. He had answered "no" where it said that he understood he'd be subject to military discipline. The court martial was dismissed.

If Britain was invaded, Turing knew the banks would fail and his money would become worthless. He converted some money into silver bars and buried the bars in the countryside to keep them safe. Unfortunately, he was never able to find them again.

Turing became friends with Joan Clarke, a fellow mathematician and code breaker. They went to the movies and biked around the countryside together. He took her home to meet his family and she introduced him to hers. He asked her to marry him. Turing was known to be honest and honorable. He told her that he had homosexual tendencies. She still agreed to marry him. Their engagement only lasted a few months. He was the one who broke it off.

NAVAL ENIGMA

Meanwhile the German Naval Enigma code was still considered unbreakable. German submarines—called U-boats—lurked in the Atlantic Ocean, preying on Allied vessels. So many British supply ships were being sunk that it was predicted that Great Britain might be starving within a few months.

Turing seized on the idea of breaking the naval code. He was delighted that no one else was working on it because then he could have it all to himself. Turing established a special unit of people, called Hut 8, to decipher the Naval Enigma Code.

He actually broke the Naval Enigma Code in one night in 1939. Turing figured out that the starting wheel positions were being encrypted twice when it was sent to the receiver of the decoded message. But knowing the method was not enough. The navy had to capture more information before Hut 8 was able to regularly decode messages and discover the location of U-boats. Once they knew where the U-boats were, though, Allied ships were able to stay away from them and travel safely across the Atlantic.

A MISSION WORTHY OF AGENT 007

The code breakers at Bletchley Park needed more informa-tion before they could reliably decode the German Naval Enigma messages. The people at British Naval Intelligence understood the urgency and Lieutenant Commander Ian Fleming came up with a plan to capture the materials that were needed. Fleming would later become famous as the author of the *James Bond, Agent 007* novels. Fleming's own plan to recover the Naval Enigma information was worthy of James Bond. He wrote the following top-secret memo to the director of Naval Intelligence.

I suggest we obtain the loot by the following means:
1. Obtain from Air Ministry an air-worthy German bomber.
2. Pick a tough crew of five, including a pilot, W/T operator and word-perfect German speaker. Dress them in German Air Force Uniform, add blood and bandages to suit.
3. Crash Plane in the Channel after making SOS to rescue service.
4. Once aboard rescue boat, shoot German crew, dump overboard, bring rescue boat back to English port.

Fleming named the mission "Operation Ruthless" and told Turing about it. Turing was enthusiastic about

Operation Ruthless and looked forward to its success. But the air force could not find an appropriate target and the mission was canceled. Turing was upset but eventually the information he needed was captured by other methods.

The Germans were aware that the Allies suddenly knew how to evade their submarines. It was important that the Germans did not know their code had been broken. To cover that fact, the British spread a rumor that Britain had developed long-range radar. The Germans believed the rumor and continued to use the Enigma code.

At this point, the code breakers at Bletchley realized they did not have enough people and machines to keep up with all the messages that needed to be decoded. They asked the government for help through the normal channels but got no response. So Turing and his colleagues wrote a letter to Prime Minister Winston Churchill and had it hand delivered to his office. After reading the letter, Churchill ordered, "ACTION THIS DAY Make sure they have all they want on extreme priority and report to me that this has been done."

Prime Minister Winston Churchill was instrumental in making sure that the Bletchley code breakers had everything they needed to help win the war.

By 1943, the Bombes at Blechley Park were decoding eighty-four thousand Enigma messages each month. Winston Churchill later said that Turing's code-breaking work might have shortened the war by as much as five years. Some military history experts would lower that estimate to two years. Either way, Turing's code-breaking work at Bletchley Park made a huge difference. Analysts have said that if the war had continued for another two to three years, as many as twenty-one million more people would have died.

Chapter Three

STAR CODE BREAKER

In 1940, the Germans began using a more sophisticated and secure code for their high-level intelligence. These coded messages carried information between Hitler and his commanders, including their plans, details of military movements, and their strengths. The code was called Tunny, but was nicknamed "Fish" by the Bletchley Park code breakers. The Tunny code was produced on a Lorenz machine.

Tunny only needed one person to code the messages. Enigma required three. When the sender typed the message into the Tunny machine, it coded the message. Morse code was not needed to send the message. It was sent directly through radio links.

The British team at Bletchley Park could not crack this code to read the intercepted messages. There were

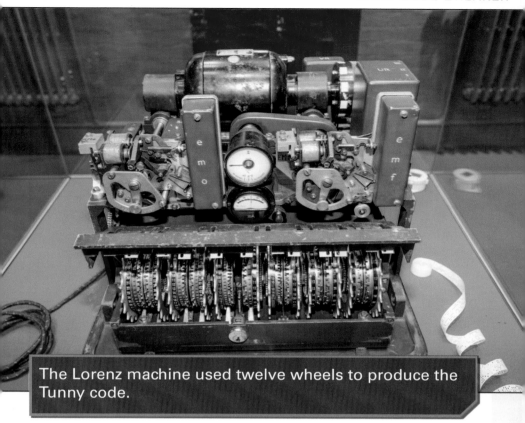

The Lorenz machine used twelve wheels to produce the Tunny code.

some breakthroughs, though. Colonel John Tiltman managed to decode one message. It took him ten days and a lot of guessing. Another man, Bill Tutte, figured out how the Lorenz machine worked. Tunny's encoding machine actually had twelve wheels. This was important information, but still no one could break the code.

Turing temporarily left Hut 8 to help the Research Section break Tunny. Once again, it was a matter of knowing the wheel details. Within a few weeks, Turing came up with a method that worked. His method was called

Turingery, and it used pencil, paper, and an eraser, not a machine. For a year British code breakers used Turingery to decode and read top-secret German messages. The messages were often from Hitler himself. Code breakers later said that Turingery changed the nature of the war and that the war might have been lost without Turing.

The ultra-secret history of the Tunny operation was kept classified until 2000. Also classified were two papers on code breaking that Turing wrote at Bletchley Park. The information in them was so top secret that the papers were not made public until April 2012.

GOING TO AMERICA

The United States entered the war in 1941, and at that point it looked like the naval battle in the Atlantic was swinging in favor of the Allies. But in February 1942 the Germans made a change and the Naval Enigma code was unbreakable again.

Turing was chosen to go to America to consult with their code breakers. He would have to travel on a passenger ship across the Atlantic with no clue

German submarines, such as *U-32*, made travel across the Atlantic dangerous. Before *U-32* was itself sunk on October 28, 1940, it sank twenty ships.

where the U-boats were waiting to attack. But a month before he was to leave, the British captured a U-boat and gained the key to the Naval Enigma. The Enigma machine had been changed so that it now used a fourth wheel. Soon the German Naval Enigma messages were being decoded again.

Turing's ship safely crossed the Atlantic Ocean and docked in New York City. After some difficulty with his paperwork, he was allowed off the ship and traveled on to Washington, D.C. Not only were the Americans deal-

THE CODE THAT WAS NEVER BROKEN

Alan Turing may not have been impressed with the American code breakers, but the Americans came up with a radio code that was never broken. In May 1942, twenty-nine Navajos were recruited by the United States Marine Corps to create a code based on their language. The Navajo language had no alphabet, no written form, and was very difficult to learn. It did not have words for military terms like *fighter plane* and *battleship*. The twenty-nine young men worked around the clock to create a code. They used everyday Navajo words to substitute for the military terms. *Hummingbird* meant fighter plane, *whale* meant battleship, and an *iron fish* was a submarine. Over four hundred military terms had to be created and memorized. The Navajo code talkers created a dictionary to help.

At first the military was skeptical. But after a successful demonstration, more Navajos were recruited and trained. The messages were transmitted over radio channels with no further encoding needed. With a Navajo code talker to send the message and another to receive it, the code was easily used. Two code talkers worked together to send and receive the messages. One person was needed to crank the portable radio. The enemy was never able to break the code.

The work of the Navajo code talkers was kept secret until 1968 when it was declassified. Congressional Gold

Medals were awarded to the original twenty-nine Navajo code talkers in 2001. This is the highest possible Congressional award. Chester Nez was one of the original twenty-nine code talkers. When he was ninety years old he said in an interview with CNN that the work of the Navajo code talkers showed "that diverse cultures can make a country richer and stronger."

ing with the Germans but also the Japanese, who had their own Enigma machines. Turing met with American code breakers and told them how to build a Bombe. From there he traveled to a factory in Ohio to advise workers as they built more than one hundred Bombes for the United States Navy. Turing was not impressed with American cryptography skills, feeling the Americans were more interested in the machines than in the thinking behind them.

Turing also visited Bell Labs where they were working on a machine for voice encryption. This work was so secret that the chief of staff of the U.S. Army said that Turing could not be allowed access. However, he was eventually allowed in and talked to the engineers about the challenges and possibilities of encoding voice transmissions. Their machine was called a vocoder. It had tall cabinets running along three sides of the room.

THE ONE-TON COMPUTER

When Turing returned to Britain in March 1943, he found the British code breakers trying to automate Turing's method of breaking the Tunny code. The Heath-Robinson machine in June 1943 was the first try, but it was unreliable. However, a new machine called Colossus was fast and reliable. It was the first all-electronic digital computing machine, and it was used to decode Tunny messages starting in February 1944. Using Colossus, five times as many Tunny messages were decoded as before. Turing did not work on Colossus. His former assistant, Tommy Flowers, developed the machine. Flowers built it in London and delivered it to Bletchley Park in the back of a truck.

Tommy Flowers was first sent to Bletchley Park to help Turing with the Enigma code. Flowers got along well with Turing and they respected each other. Turing recommended Flowers when Max Newman was having trouble constructing his Heath-Robinson machine for decoding Tunny.

Flowers thought a faster, more reliable machine could be built. When he first proposed the idea of an all-electronic machine using one to two thousand vacuum tubes (called "valves" in Britain) everyone pointed out that vacuum tubes were not reliable in large numbers. But Flowers believed that if the vacuum tubes were left turned on they wouldn't explode, as they usually did when turned on and off.

Tommy Flowers and his team worked day and night in his London laboratory to build a computer that would quickly break the Tunny-coded messages. He was lucky that his boss in the Post Office engineering research laboratories gave him whatever he needed. He received no help from the people at Bletchley Park.

It took ten months to build Colossus. Colossus was huge, taking up an entire room and weighing a ton. When Flowers took Colossus to Bletchley, everyone was amazed at how fast it was. Within two weeks it was set to work on Tunny. Information was inputted on punched paper tape. When things went wrong, the tape shredded and shot out everywhere. A manual typewriter delivered the output of the machine. The typewriter had rods attached to its keys leading to the machine. That way it would type the decoded information on its own.

Colossus was astonishingly fast. It has been compared to the speed of the first home computers, although it was much, much bigger. Colossus also gave off an incredible amount of heat. In the winter, the Wrens and the engineers operating the machine welcomed the warmth. Fuel and food shortages meant that there was little heat in the huts or the living quarters and the food was poor.

Colossus had to be programmed by changing plugs and switches. It was a time-consuming process as the women changed the wiring according to new instructions. Turing had written a paper about storing programs

These are the control panels of Colossus, which was operated by Wrens who manually changed the plugs and switches.

in a computer's memory, but Flowers said he didn't understand it. So Colossus was programmed by hand.

Colossus was an enormous success. By spring 1944, Churchill and the War Cabinet were demanding that Flowers build twelve more Colossus machines. They ordered that it be given the highest priority, but Flowers said his team was already working as hard as they could.

He could only promise one more machine by June. He delivered it in time for D-Day (June 6, 1944). Although Turing did not work on the machine itself, his statistical methods were the basis for the techniques used in Colossus.

BUILDING DELILAH

Turing declined the chance to work more on Tunny and, in fall 1943, he left Bletchley Park. He moved ten miles (16 km) away to Hanslope Park, another old mansion used by the Special Communications Unit Number 3. This unit researched ways to send coded messages.

Turing wanted to work on a secure way to encode the human voice using electronic techniques he had seen at Bell Labs. The sound waves of speech could not be turned into Morse code or another method where letters are encoded. Turing planned to build a vocoder, a machine that would turn sound waves into something that sounded like static. He called his machine Delilah. It was the size of three shoeboxes, unlike the machine at Bell Labs that took up three sides of a room.

People celebrated in the streets of London when the war in Europe ended on May 7, 1945. The Australian serviceman in the front is carrying an Australian flag.

While he worked at Hanslope, Turing ate his meals with the soldiers there and lived in a cottage nearby. He had two assistants, Robin Gandy and Don Bayley, and became good friends with them. When he heard that the soldiers were having a one-mile (1.6-km) race, he entered. Some of the men thought he was joking, but he was still an excellent runner. He easily beat everyone else.

In 1944, Turing successfully encoded a speech by Churchill. The speech sounded like static but when it was decoded it was understandable again. However, Delilah had some technical problems, and it was not ready to go until spring 1945. Unfortunately for Turing, it was not put to use. On May 7, 1945, Germany surrendered and the war in Europe was over.

Chapter Four

BUILDING A BRAIN

Even after the war in Europe was over, the work Alan Turing had done continued to be top secret. Very few people knew of the valuable work he and the other code breakers had done. In June 1945 he was secretly awarded the Order of the British Empire (OBE), which honors those who have given distinguished service to Britain.

Although Turing accepted the award, he seems not to have valued it highly. His brother, John, said he kept it in a tin box along with his screws, nails, nuts, and bolts.

Now that the war was over, Turing was thinking again about his universal computing machine, the Turing Machine first mentioned in his 1936 paper. Since his Cambridge days he had learned a lot about electronics

Turing became an Officer of the Most Excellent Order of the British Empire (OBE) when he was awarded this medal.

and designing digital machines. He talked to friends about building a "brain" and had even discussed it at Bell Labs a few years earlier. He said then that it did not have to be a powerful brain, only a barely adequate brain like that of the president of AT&T. Bell Labs was owned by AT&T.

COMPUTER WARS

In October 1945 Turing went to work at the National Physical Laboratory (NPL) in London. NPL focused on research and hoped to be the first to design and construct an electronic computing machine with stored programs.

However, the American electronic computer ENIAC was completed first and there was no other computer like it. But the early ENIAC was hard to program. By February 1946, Turing had designed an electronic computer called the Automatic Computing

Engine, or ACE. Turing felt that the ACE was far ahead of ENIAC. ACE stored programs in its memory. Turing focused on making the machine as fast as possible. He said that not only was speed necessary but a large memory was also necessary if the machine was going to be capable of more than trivial operations. The instruction tables he wrote for ACE are considered an early computer

The Pilot ACE computer, which was built in 1950, was based on, but did not exactly follow, Turing's design.

programming language.

But ACE, as designed by Turing, was never built. (A modified version was built in 1950.) NPL did not have the funding to carry through. Don Bayley, the engineer who had worked with Turing on Delilah, said that Turing had gone to the NPL thinking he was going to make an electronic brain. Then, after several months working out the design of the ACE, he was told he could not make it. Turing was offended that they employed him to make a brain and then did not let him do it. The NPL also expected him to attend meetings and fill out paperwork, all of which he felt took time away from his real work.

Perhaps due to his frustration, Turing took up running again. He trained cross-country and ran to his meetings. Turing often beat those who took public transportation. He was considered a serious candidate for the British 1948 Olym-

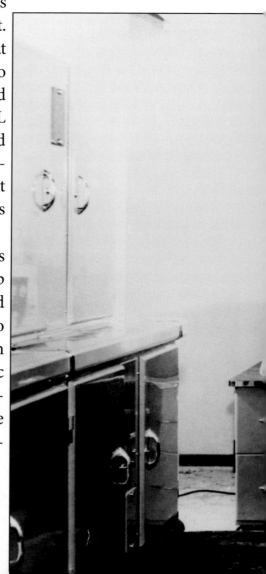

pic team until he injured his hip and could no longer run competitively.

In fall 1947, Turing took a sabbatical, or paid time away, from NPL. He went to Cambridge for a year. He wrote a groundbreaking paper on neural nets and submitted it to NPL. It was never published in his lifetime. When his sabbatical year ended, Turing left NPL for the

Turing is conferring with colleagues from the University of Manchester on the Ferranti Mark 1 computer in this photograph from 1951.

University of Manchester—in the city of Manchester, in northwestern England—to become the deputy director of its Royal Society Computing Machine Laboratory. He designed an input-output system and wrote programs for its Manchester Baby computer. He also wrote a programming manual, the first in the world. The Manchester Baby was improved into the Ferranti Mark 1, the world's first electronic digital computer to be sold commercially.

CAN A MACHINE THINK?

Turing was interested in developing a machine that could do more than calculate. He wanted to create a thinking machine. But he was not sure how to define intelligence in a machine. He thought that perhaps the game of chess might be a good test. He wrote instructions for a computer to carry out but no computer was powerful enough to run the program. So Turing pretended to be the computer and followed his own instructions while playing a chess game with a friend. Turing called his program Turochamp, but his friend emerged as the champ of their game. However, when he played another friend's wife, Turochamp won.

Turing continued to explore the concept of computer intelligence. In his 1950 article, "Computing Machinery and Intelligence," he asks the question, "Can machines think?" A few sentences later, though, Turing says the question is absurd. Instead he says he would replace the question with a new form of the problem, one that could be described in terms of a game.

He went on to describe the Imitation Game, in which he proposed criteria for whether a machine could be called intelligent. In the Imitation Game, which became known as the Turing Test, one person tried to decide which parts of a written conversation were from a human and which from a computer.

The conversation would consist of questions and answers. The computer would need to be programmed to answer the way a human would. It might take a long time to do math and it might make mistakes. It would also have to give a human-type response if it could not answer the question. It could even say "no" if it was asked if it was a computer. Turing gave the following examples in his paper. In the second question the computer has purposefully answered the math problem wrong.

Q: Please write me a sonnet on the subject of the Forth Bridge.
A: Count me out on this one. I never could write poetry.

Q: Add 34957 to 70764.
A: (Pause about 30 seconds and then give as answer) 105621.

EUGENE AND THE TURING TEST

In 2014, many people believed that a computer had finally passed the Turing Test. During an annual Turing Test in London, a computer convinced 33 percent of its questioners that it was human. Four other computers failed to convince even 30 percent that they were human. The winning computer identified itself to the questioners as a thirteen-year-old Ukrainian boy named Eugene Goostman. In reality, Eugene was the brainchild of two Russian adults.

Some people criticized the claim that Eugene passed the Turing Test. They said that five minutes of questions was not enough. Another complaint was that pretending to be a child who did not speak English very well was not a fair way to pass the test. One professor who heard that Eugene had passed called it nonsense, saying, "We have not passed the Turing Test. We are not even close."

After the test, transcripts of an earlier 2012 "conversation" with Eugene were made available, including the porting on the facing page, which was reprinted in the London *Telegraph*. The word "entity," which means a "being," refers to Eugene here.

Judge: Hi, I'm Cathy.
Entity: Cathy! Nice to meet you! You're a woman, if I'm not mistaken.

Judge: Right. What is your name?
Entity: People call me Eugene. Or "Zhenya." It is a short name for Eugene in Russia and Ukraine.

Judge: Nice name. Are you from either area?
Entity: Agree :-) Oh, what a fruitful conversation;-)

Judge: Do you really think so?
Entity: No, your guess was wrong. I don't think so. By the way, I still don't know your specialty—or, possibly, I've missed it?

Judge: What specialty? What's yours?
Entity: Huh? And I forgot to ask you where you are from...

Judge: The universe and you?
Entity: Is it your hobby to ask little poor Jewish boys such tricky questions they don't have an answer for?

> *Q: Do you play chess?*
> *A: Yes.*
> *Q: I have K at my K1, and no other pieces. You have only K at K6 and R at R1. It is your move. What do you play?*
> *A: (After a pause of 15 seconds) R-R8 mate.*

Turing stated that within fifty years (the year 2000), computer programming would advance to the point that computers would be able to fool questioners 30 percent of the time. After five minutes, he thought the average questioner would have a 70 percent chance of correctly identifying the computer. Later, in 1952 he changed his estimate to say that it would be at least a hundred years before a computer could pass the test.

People have raised objections to the validity of the Turing Test. But it is still probably the most famous method of testing computer intelligence. Because of his work in this field, Turing is sometimes called the father of artificial intelligence.

In 1951, Alan Turing became a Fellow of the Royal Society. Members of the Royal Society must be elected based on their work and are considered to be the world's most outstanding scientists.

At this point Turing had turned his attention to a new field of study—mathematical biology. He was interested in why and how patterns in nature happened.

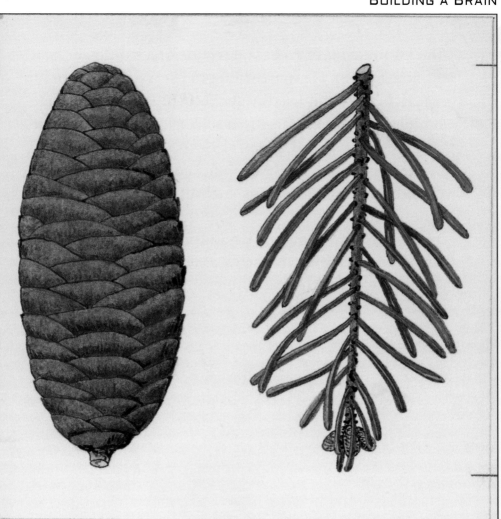

Abies concolor

Turing's new field of study was mathematical biology, here seen in the patterns of a pinecone.

The numeric patterns of a pinecone or a sunflower head fascinated him. He was the first to use a computer in his research when he used Manchester's Ferranti to make simulations of growing tissue. In 1952 Turing submitted his paper "The Chemical Basis of Morphogenesis" to the Royal Society. It was another pioneering paper, though it was not seen as such at the time. Morphogenesis—the subject of Turing's paper—is the process by which plants, animals, and other living things grow and develop. Turing himself was especially interested in symmetry in nature and in how stripes, spots, and other patterns develop.

Chapter Five

TRIAL, CONVICTION, DEATH

Although Turing did not keep his homosexuality a secret from friends, not everyone knew about it. Homosexuality was a crime in Britain at that time. I. J. Good, who worked with Turing at Bletchley Park and the University of Manchester, said in an interview for the BBC TV science series *Horizon*, "It was probably a good thing that the security people did not know because he might then have been fired and we might have lost the war."

ARRESTED AND CONVICTED

In 1952, Turing reported a break-in at his home. The police caught the thief, but discovered Turing was gay. Turing was arrested for gross indecency. Some say that if he had denied it, the charges would probably have been

Alan Turing was persecuted for his sexual orientation. Though we now recognize that this was wrong, it was very common at the time.

dropped. But he admitted it and was convicted. His lawyer asked that he be spared a prison sentence, saying that he was doing important work. The judge agreed, sentencing Turing to a year's probation, plus a series of chemical treatments that were supposed to reduce his sex drive. The treatment consisted of estrogen injections and was also known as chemical castration.

Now that he was known to be homosexual, there was a fear that enemy agents would try to blackmail him about government secrets. Turing had continued his secret work with the Govern-

This is University of Manchester's College of Technology in 1952. Alan Turing continued to work there after his conviction for indecency.

ment Communications Headquarters (GCHQ), formerly known as Bletchley Park's Government Code and Cypher School. Not only had he learned top-secret information during the war, he also now knew about current secret

SPIES AMONG US

After World War II ended, international tensions remained high. The United States and Britain feared that their former ally, the Soviet Union, would permanently take over Eastern Europe and expand its power into more countries. The Soviet Union was determined that Germany would never again threaten it. It wanted to spread communism into other countries. The hostilities among the countries were called the Cold War, although actual war was never declared and weapons were rarely used.

Each side developed networks of spies. Many of the Russian spies were recruited from the British and American people. Russian citizens were recruited by the Americans and the British, too. This made each side distrustful of its own people. If the government thought someone could be recruited or blackmailed into spying, that person was kept from important jobs and watched. Homosexuals were seen as especially open to blackmail. This is why Turing's ability to work on top-secret government projects was taken away.

One spy group in particular may have made the government nervous about Turing. In 1951, five men in high positions in the British government were discovered to be part of a spy ring. The men were Cambridge graduates, like Turing, and the spy ring was called the Cambridge Five. The men worked in intelligence, security, and the Foreign Office. They betrayed many high-level government secrets. Although the ring was exposed, none of them was ever prosecuted.

projects. After his arrest, Turing's security clearance was canceled and he was banned from continuing his government work.

Turing's contract at the University of Manchester was renewed so he was able to continue his work on artificial intelligence and biology. Some of his friends felt the arrest and treatment had not affected him very much, saying he bore it with "amused fortitude." The police continued to watch him and he called them "poor sweeties" to his friends.

Other people thought the fact that he had lost his government clearance was distressing to him. It meant that he could no longer continue the kind of secret work that he had enjoyed.

In 1953, Turing's year of probation and treatments was up. He continued to investigate patterns of growth at the University of Manchester and traveled to France and Greece on vacation.

DEATH

On June 8, 1954, two years after Turing's conviction and a year after the treatments were finished, his housekeeper returned from a weekend holiday. She found Alan Turing in bed, dead of cyanide poisoning at the age of forty-one. He lay neatly in his bed, a partially eaten apple beside him.

Turing had been conducting experiments in the room next to his bedroom. He had a quantity of potassium cyanide there, used in an experiment that involved electroplating.

Turing's brother, John, was advised not to bring a lawyer to the inquest. An inquest is a legal inquiry by a coroner or medical examiner into the cause of death. John was told there was little chance of the death being ruled an accident. John followed the advice and Alan Turing's death was ruled a suicide.

Turing's mother was in Italy and was not able to return in time for the inquest. She felt that John had mishandled the inquest and that there should have been a proper investigation. But John firmly believed the death was a suicide and he had done the right thing.

NOT A SUICIDE?

Despite the coroner's verdict of suicide, many believed Turing's death was an accident, including his mother.

SOCRATES, SNOW WHITE, AND THE APPLE LOGO

The manner of Alan Turing's death, involving poison and a half-eaten apple, has inspired comparisons to other events. Many people connect Turing with the Greek philosopher Socrates. Like Turing, Socrates was highly intelligent and often angered those in authority. Socrates liked to wander the streets, discussing and debating philosophical questions with people he met. The young people of Athens were especially open to talking to him. Socrates was accused of corrupting the youths. He expressed no regrets, was sentenced to death, and died by drinking a cup of hemlock. Neither Socrates nor Turing argued his innocence when accused, nor did either argue against the unfair punishment.

There are people who believe Alan Turing's death was inspired by a Disney villain. Turing was fascinated with the movie *Snow White and the Seven Dwarfs*. The movie was shown in Cambridge in 1938 and Turing was struck by the scene where the Evil Queen transforms into the witch. She offers Snow White an apple—poison on one side and clean on the other. According to the article "Alan Turing, My Hero," by Turing's running partner, Alan Garner, Turing "used to go over the scene in detail, dwelling on the ambiguity of the apple, red on one side, green on

(continued on page 72)

(continued from page 71)

the other, one of which gave death." A co-worker said Turing walked the halls quoting the movie lines, "Dip the apple in the brew, let the sleeping death seep through." Some say he was inspired by the movie to use an apple in his suicide.

One urban legend says that the Apple computer logo is a reference to Turing. The logo is an apple with a bite taken out of it. Rob Janoff, the designer of the Apple logo, discussed his design in an interview with Ivan Raszl for the website creativebits.org. Janoff talked about the legends surrounding the logo and Turing. He mentioned all the "cool" connections to Turing's life that people see in the logo. From 1977 to 1998 the apple had rainbow stripes on it. Some people thought the colored stripes on the logo were a reference to the gay pride flag since Turing was gay. And of course, there was an apple with a bite in it found beside Turing's bedside.

Janoff said the real reason the apple has a bite out of it "is kind of a letdown." He says it was a matter of scale, so that the apple would not look like a cherry. Not being a computer person, he did not even know about Turing when he designed the logo. He was even surprised to hear that people think the bite a play on the computer term "byte." He had never heard of a byte until his creative director told him about it.

However, others argued that he had arranged his suicide so that his mother could believe that it was an accident.

His mother pointed out that Turing was always careless and untidy with his experiments and he could have accidentally breathed in some cyanide gas. There was no suicide note, he had no financial worries, and she had seen no signs of depression.

Others agreed that suicide was unlikely, including the housekeeper and neighbors. His neighbor Mrs. Webb said she'd seen him a few days earlier and he was "very jolly." He had made notes about future plans, such as buying theater tickets and new socks. He had left a note on his desk at work about the tasks he wanted to do when he returned after the weekend. The week before his death, he had discussed writing a paper with a colleague and meeting in a few months in Cambridge.

Turing was known to eat an apple before bedtime, so it was not unusual to find a partially eaten one beside his bed. The apple itself was never actually tested for cyanide. If Turing had eaten an apple laced with cyanide, traces of the poison should have been found in his liver. However, the pathologist's report said his liver was normal. Turing's psychiatrist wrote to his mother in January 1955, "There is not the slightest doubt to me that Alan died by an accident."

Some people wonder if the government had Turing killed because he knew top-secret information. Perhaps

Guy Burgess was part of the Cambridge Five. He passed information along to the Soviets while he was working for British Intelligence.

he was considered to be a security risk. However, no concrete evidence has been found to support this theory. That said, his housekeeper did mention a strange fact. She found his shoes outside his bedroom door, as if they'd been left there to be polished. This was a practice of people who had servants. But Turing had no servant to polish his shoes and had never left his shoes there before.

Those who think the government was involved say that officials may have been more nervous than usual around the time of Turing's death. They point out that a few months earlier a Soviet spy ring had been discovered involving graduates of Cambridge. Two of the men, one of whom was gay, took refuge in the Soviet Union. It seems unlikely that anyone will ever be able to prove or fully disprove the theories surrounding Turing's death.

Alan Turing left an enduring legacy in the sciences. But his brother, John, said that many people who knew him personally also remembered Alan Turing for his modesty, his generosity, and his kindness. Both John and his mother quoted Turing's old headmaster's tribute in his school magazine after his death:

For those who knew him here the memory is of an even-tempered, lovable character with an impish sense of humour and a modesty proof against all achievements. ... In all his preoccupation with logic, mathematics, and science he never lost his common touch; in a short life he accomplished much, and to the roll of great names in the history of his particular studies added his own.

Chapter Six

FAMOUS AFTER DEATH

Today Alan Turing is remembered as a pioneer of computer science, a first researcher in both artificial intelligence and artificial life, and a code breaker whose work helped shorten World War II.

ALAN TURING'S LEGACY

The concept of modern computers is often said to be based on Turing's 1936 paper, "On Computable Numbers, with an Application to the Entscheidungsproblem." In the paper he described his Universal Turing Machine, which could be programmed to compute and perform any well-defined tasks. The Universal Turing Machine was theoretical, but it is described as the foundation for computing.

This life-sized statue at Bletchley Park shows Turing sitting at an Enigma machine. The statue is made of pieces of Welsh slate.

Alan Turing
1912 - 1954
Mathematician - codebreaker
Stephen Kettle 2007

His Turing Test is still considered a benchmark for testing computer intelligence. The test requires a computer to hold a "conversation" with a judge without the judge realizing he or she is not dealing with a computer. Some people feel the Turing Test was finally passed in 2014; others say there is a long way to go before computers can pass the test. Turing's contributions helped define and demonstrate artificial intelligence.

Turing's code-breaking work had to remain secret during World War II and long after. He received little recognition for that work until long after his death. However, he did secretly receive an OBE for his code-breaking work during his lifetime.

With the declassification of the Enigma operation in the 1970s, Alan Turing's code-breaking efforts in World War II could finally be recognized. The stories of Tunny and Colossus were not released until 2000. Also classified were two papers on code breaking that Turing had written while he was at Bletchley. Their information was so secret that the papers were not made public until April 2012.

By the early twenty-first century, the recognitions began to mount up. In a 2013 interview with the British newspaper *The Daily Mail*, Alan Turing's niece Inagh Payne said, "Alan never had any recognition in his lifetime. I hope he realises the recognition he's getting now. … But he'd be shy about it. He didn't want an awful lot of fuss."

BLETCHLEY PARK SECRETS

The story of the work that Alan Turing and his fellow code breakers did at Bletchley Park remained secret until the 1970s. By the 1990s the buildings were in terrible shape. They were saved from being demolished when the Bletchley Park Trust was formed to make the site into a museum.

The British National Museum of Computing was established there. Visitors can see replicas of the Enigma-breaking Bombe machine, as well as of Colossus, the machine that was used to crack the Tunny code.

In 2013, new secrets were uncovered at Bletchley. But in typical Bletchley fashion, the news was not released until 2015. While renovating the huts that are scattered on the grounds, workers discovered top-secret papers written by the code breakers. All paperwork and other evidence of their code-breaking work was supposed to have been destroyed. So these papers are a rare glimpse into the important wartime work at Bletchley.

Turing and the other code breakers worked in the huts, which were very cold in the winter. These papers, apparently old notes and work papers, had been crumpled up and stuffed into the ceilings and holes in the walls to keep out the cold. It is an indication of how primitive the working conditions were in the huts.

(continued on page 80)

(continued from page 79)

The dozens of handwritten sheets are covered in letters and numbers, crossed out, checked off, or grouped together. They show how the code breakers worked on the coded messages. The writers used both pencils and crayons. Experts were especially excited to find the only known examples of Banbury sheets. These sheets use one of the techniques that Turing came up with to speed up code breaking. Banbury sheets have holes punched in them and, when they are slid across each other, a light will shine through matching holes. This method helped with the solving of the Naval Enigma code.

As soon as the papers were discovered, they were frozen to preserve them. Later they were thawed out and carefully cleaned and repaired. Then they were put on display in a special exhibition.

RECOGNITIONS, AWARDS, AND HONORS

In the decades after his death, Alan Turing has received many awards and honors. A few of them include:

- 1966, the A. M. Turing Award in computer science was established by the Association for Computing Machinery. This award is sometimes called the Nobel Prize of computing.
- 1999, Turing was named one of the "100 Most Important People of the 20th Century" by *Time* magazine. It said, "everyone who taps at a keyboard, opening a spreadsheet or a word-processing program, is working on an incarnation of a Turing machine."
- 2001, a statue of Turing sitting on a bench was unveiled on his birthday, June 23. A plaque at his feet reads, "Father of computer science, mathematician, logician, wartime codebreaker, victim of prejudice."
- 2002, a BBC poll named Turing one of the "100 Greatest Britons."
- 2004, Turing was named the second-most significant alumnus of Princeton University.
- 2004, a historical marker, called a Blue Plaque, was placed on the site of Turing's birthplace in London.
- 2005, a new science center at Bletchley Park was dedicated to Turing.
- 2007, a life-sized statue of Turing was installed at Bletchley Park.
- 2007, the University of Manchester renamed a building complex the Alan Turing Building.
- 2012, another Blue Plaque was placed at King's College, Cambridge, in Turing's memory.

To celebrate the centenary of Turing's birth, 2012 was declared Alan Turing Year in Britain. Many exhibits, projects, and performances celebrated Turing's life during that year. As part of the centenary celebrations, London's Science Museum had an exhibition about Turing's life and work. An Alan Turing Monopoly game was marketed by Bletchley Park, and Britain put out an Alan

This is the Alan Turing Building at the University of Manchester. It houses the School of Mathematics and the Centre for Astrophysics.

Turing commemorative stamp. Thousands of people participated in the Turing Sunflower Project to gather data for further research into one of Turing's theories. A musical composition, *A Man from the Future*, was performed at the Royal Albert Hall in London. It was inspired by Turing's life and work.

THE TURING SUNFLOWER PROJECT

Turing's paper on the mathematical basis for patterns in nature sparked a special kind of research project in 2012. One hundred years after his birth, scientists, ordinary citizens, and schoolchildren joined together to gather evidence to test Turing's theories.

Turing wanted to find out why sunflower seeds and petals follow a mathematical pattern. He had observed this pattern in the sunflowers in his own garden. This pattern is called the Fibonacci sequence. In the sequence, each number is the sum of the previous two numbers. The sequence starts 0, 1, 1, 2, 3, 5, 8, 13, and so on.

The sequence does not only apply to sunflowers. Pinecones, uncurling ferns, roses, and other plants demonstrate the sequence. Turing drew on his obser-

Thousands of people gathered data from sunflower heads, such as this one, to test Turing's theories of morphogenesis.

vation of plants to come up with his own theory of morphogenesis. It was later shown that even the patterns of spots and stripes on animals and fish fit into Turing's theories.

As part of the celebrations to honor Alan Turing one hundred years after his birth, Professor Jonathan Swinton came up with the idea that people all over the world could grow sunflowers and count the spirals. He thought Turing's idea was correct but wanted data to confirm it. So the Turing Sunflower Project was born.

The Manchester Science Festival, the University of Manchester, and the Museum of Science and Industry, Manchester, all joined in the experiment. They hoped that many people would grow sunflowers, allowing them to collect a large set of data with which to test Turing's theories.

Thousands of people from seven countries contributed data. They sent in measurements and recorded the number of spirals in their sunflower heads. They also described whether the spiral ran clockwise or counterclockwise.

Eighty-two percent of the sunflowers followed the Fibonacci sequence. Professor Swinton said in the *Manchester Evening News* that this proves Alan Turing's observations. This data could help biologists understand the growth of plants.

TURING ON STAGE AND SCREEN

A play, documentaries, and several movies have been written and performed about Turing's life. In 1987, the play *Breaking the Code* was written by Hugh Whitemore. The British actor Derek Jacobi played Alan Turing in the play. He was nominated for three Tony Awards.

The movie *Codebreaker* (its British title was *Britain's Greatest Codebreaker*) was released in 2011. The movie's writers included statements they said were from Turing's psychiatrist. However, the statements contradict what the psychiatrist actually said to Turing's mother about his death—that he believed Turing's death was an accident, not a suicide.

The 2014 movie *The Imitation Game* was a huge success and introduced Alan Turing to a wider audience. Stars Benedict Cumberbatch and Keira Knightley were both nominated for Best Performance Oscars. Overall the movie won fifty-two awards, including an Oscar for the Best Adapted Screenplay, and was nominated for 124 more awards.

APOLOGY AND PARDON

Alan Turing was convicted of gross indecency for being a homosexual, which was a crime at that time. His punishment was to undergo a series of chemical injections.

This is the movie poster from *The Imitation Game*, which starred Benedict Cumberbatch as Alan Turing.

BEHIND EVERY CODE IS AN ENIGMA

BENEDICT CUMBERBATCH — KEIRA KNIGHTLEY
THE IMITATION GAME
COMING SOON

In 2009, thousands of Britons signed a petition asking for an apology for Turing's horrible treatment by the justice system. The petition received support from around the world.

Gordon Brown, who was Great Britain's prime minister at that time, made a public apology in the British newspaper *The Telegraph*. Brown's apology was titled, "I'm Proud to Say Sorry to a Real War Hero." In his apology, Brown acknowledged Turing's many achievements, saying, "He truly was one of those individuals we can point to whose unique contribution helped to turn the tide of war. The debt of gratitude he is owed makes it all the more horrifying, therefore, that he was treated so inhumanely." Brown ended the apology with the words, "So on behalf of the British government, and all those who live freely thanks to Alan's work, I am very proud to say: we're sorry. You deserved so much better."

Later, the British justice secretary, Chris Grayling, requested that the queen issue a formal pardon to Alan Turing. Royal pardons are rare, but on December 24, 2013, Queen Elizabeth issued a formal pardon. Grayling told *The Telegraph*, "Dr. Turing deserves to be remembered and recognised for his fantastic contribution to the war effort and his legacy to science. A pardon from the Queen is a fitting tribute to an exceptional man."

522,619: Pardon all men convicted like Alan Turing

Change.org/Pardon49000Men

s grandnephew, grandniece, and great-great
w presented a petition to the prime minister, asking
her convicted homosexuals be pardoned, in 2015.

In 2015, relatives of Alan Turing presented a petition asking that the forty-nine thousand other convicted homosexuals also be pardoned. A month later the British Labour Party said that a future Labour government would introduce "Turing's Law." It would offer pardons for those convicted under the old indecency laws. Turing's great-niece said that she was sure Turing would have wanted justice for everybody. Alan Turing was a genius and a pioneer in many fields, but above all, he was human.

Timeline

1912 Alan Mathison Turing is born on June 23 in London, England.

1930 Alan's friend Christopher Morcom dies of bovine tuberculosis.

1934 Turing graduates from King's College, Cambridge University, with a degree in mathematics.

1935 Turing, age twenty-two, is elected a Fellow of King's College, Cambridge.

1936 "On Computable Numbers, with an Application to the Entscheidungsproblem" is published. In this paper Turing discusses the Turing Machine.

1938 Turing receives his Ph.D. from Princeton University in Princeton, New Jersey.

1939 Britain goes to war against Nazi Germany and Turing joins the Government Code and Cypher School at Bletchley Park to work full-time as a code breaker.

1939–1942 Turing designs a machine called the Bombe. It is used to decode the German Enigma messages throughout the war. He would also be instrumental in breaking the Naval Enigma code used to communicate with German submarines.

1942 In November, Turing travels to the United States to give advice on code breaking and building Bombes.

1943 Turing goes to Henslope Park and works on a voice encryption and communication machine called Delilah.

1945 The war in Europe ends and Turing is secretly awarded the Order of the British Empire (OBE) for his code-breaking efforts during the war. He is recruited by the National Physical Laboratory in London.

1946 Turing designs an electronic computer with stored programs called the Automatic Computing Engine, or ACE.

1948 Turing becomes Deputy Director of the Computing Laboratory at the University of Manchester.

1950 Turing publishes "Computing Machinery and Intelligence," in which he proposes the Turing Test be used to determine whether a machine can be called intelligent.

1951 Turing is elected a Fellow of the Royal Society.

1952 Turing is arrested for gross indecency and loses his security clearance.

1954 Turing is found dead of cyanide poisoning on June 7.

2014 Turing receives a posthumous royal pardon from Queen Elizabeth.

Glossary

Allies The countries, including the United States, Great Britain, and Russia, that fought against the Axis Powers in World War II.

artificial intelligence The ability of a computer to imitate human thinking and behavior.

Axis Powers The countries that fought against the Allies in World War II. The Axis countries were Germany, Italy, and Japan.

cipher A method to keep information secret by replacing a letter with another letter, a number, or a symbol. Also spelled "cypher."

colossus Someone or something that is huge or important.

cryptanalysis The study and methods of breaking codes and ciphers.

declassify To make information or documents available to everyone by removing official restrictions.

decode To change a coded message into ordinary writing.

digital In computer science, to display information in numbers.

electronic Using electricity and parts like vacuum tubes and transistors.

encode To change a message into code.

enigma A puzzle or something that cannot be easily explained.

homosexual A person who is attracted to people of the same sex.

intelligence The ability to learn and make decisions. It also means information about an enemy.

logician A person who is good at logic or reasoning.

program A set of instructions that tell a computer how to perform a particular task.

sabbatical Time given away from a job, often for the purpose of research.

U-boat A German submarine. The name is translated and shortened from the original German term meaning "undersea boat."

ultra To go to the extreme. Used with top secret to mean extremely top secret.

vacuum tube A sealed glass tube that used to be used in radios and other electronic equipment. It has mostly been replaced by transistors.

For More Information

International Spy Museum
800 F Street NW
Washington, DC 20004
(202) 393-7798
Website: http://www.spymuseum.org
   The International Spy Museum provides many
   educational resources, including games to learn
   about codes and spy vocabulary, and the stories
   behind many historical espionage cases.

Mensa Canada Society
P.O. Box 1570
Kingston, ON K7L 5C8
Canada
(613) 547-0824
Website: http://www.mensacanada.org
Mensa is an international organization for people
   who have high IQs. It promotes studies of intel-
   ligence. The group's website includes puzzles and
   games, as well as information about scholarships.

Museum of Science and Industry
5700 S. Lake Shore Drive
Chicago, IL 60637

(773) 684-1414

Website: http://www.msichicago.org

The Museum of Science and Industry is an interactive museum with exhibits that include Numbers in Nature, Robot Revolution, a real Enigma machine, and a German submarine in which you can walk around.

National Cryptologic Museum

Fort Meade, MD 20755

(301) 688-5849

Website: https://www.nsa.gov/about/cryptologic_heritage/museum/index.shtml

Part of the National Security Agency, the National Cryptologic Museum houses objects and stories about codes and code breaking, including an Enigma machine. It is the first and only public museum in the U.S. Intelligence community.

National Museum of American History

14th Street and Constitution Avenue NW

Washington, DC 20001

(202) 633-1000

Website: http://americanhistory.si.edu

The National Museum of American History is part
   of the Smithsonian. Along with other historic
   exhibits, it houses a collection of historic computers and business machines, including the ENIAC.

Ontario Science Center
770 Don Mills Road
Toronto, ON M3C 1T3
Canada
(888) 696-1110
Website: http://www.ontariosciencecentre.ca
The Ontario Science Center has interactive exhibits
   and activities, including a radio booth. The website has many online activities and virtual tours.

WEBSITES

Because of the changing nature of Internet links,
Rosen Publishing has developed an online list of
websites related to the subject of this book. This site
is updated regularly. Please use this link to access
the list:

http://www.rosenlinks.com/TP/Turing

For Further Reading

Adams, Simon, and Andy Crawford. *World War II (Eyewitness)*. Revised ed. New York, NY: DK, 2014.

Atwood, Kathryn J., and Sarah Olson. *Women Heroes of World War II: 26 Stories of Espionage, Sabotage, Resistance, and Rescue*. Chicago, IL: Chicago Review Press, 2011.

Bascomb, Neal. *The Nazi Hunters: How a Team of Spies and Survivors Captured the World's Most Notorious Nazi*. New York, NY: Scholastic, 2013.

Blumenthal, Karen. *Steve Jobs: The Man Who Thought Different: A Biography*. New York, NY: Feiwel and Friends, 2012.

Ceruzzi, Paul E. *Computing: A Concise History* (The MIT Press Essential Knowledge Series). Cambridge, MA: MIT Press, 2012.

Colson, Mary. *Destroy after Reading: The World of Secret Codes*. Chicago, IL: Raintree, 2011.

Cornioley, Pearl Witherington, and Herve Larroque. *Code Name Pauline: Memoirs of a World War II Special Agent*. Chicago, IL: Chicago Review Press, 2013.

Curley, Robert. *Architects of the Information Age*. New York, NY: Britannica Educational Publishing, 2012.

Darman, Peter. *The Battle of the Atlantic: Naval Warfare from 1939–1945*. New York, NY: Rosen Publishing, 2012.

Frauenfelder, Mark. *The Computer: An Illustrated History from Its Origins to the Present Day*. Reprint ed. London, England: Carlton Books, 2013.

Henderson, Harry. *The Digital Age*. San Diego, CA: ReferencePoint Press, 2013.

Hillenbrand, Laura. *Unbroken: An Olympian's Journey from Airman to Castaway to Captive* (The Young Adult Adaptation). New York, NY: Delacorte, 2014.

Hoose, Phillip. *The Boys Who Challenged Hitler: Knud Pedersen and the Churchill Club*. New York, NY: Farrar, Straus and Giroux (BYR), 2015.

Johnson, Bud. *Break the Code: Cryptography for Beginners*. Mineola, NY: Dover Publications, 2013.

Karam, P. Andrew. *Artificial Intelligence* (Science Foundations). New York, NY: Chelsea House Publications, 2012.

Lynch, Chris. *Dead in the Water*. New York, NY: Scholastic, 2014.

McKay, Sinclair. *The Lost World of Bletchley Park: The Illustrated History of the Wartime Codebreaking Centre*. New York, NY: Aurum Press, 2013.

McKay, Sinclair. *The Secret Lives of Codebreakers: The Men and Women Who Cracked the Enigma Code at Bletchley Park*. New York, NY: Plume, 2012.

Nez, Chester, and Judith Schiess Avila. *Code Talker*. New York, NY: Berkley Caliber, 2011.

Padua, Sydney. *The Thrilling Adventures of Lovelace and Babbage: The (Mostly) True Story of the First Computer*. London, England: Penguin Books, 2015.

Philosophy, Invention, and Engineering (Great Scientists). Redding, CT: Brown Bear, 2010.

Royston, Angela. *Inventors Who Changed the World*. New York, NY: Crabtree Publishing, 2011.

Wein, Elizabeth. *Code Name Verity*. New York, NY: Hyperion, 2012.

Bibliography

"Alan Turing." BBC. Retrieved March 22, 2015 (http://www.bbc.co.uk/history/people/alan_turing).

"Alan Turing." Bio.com. A&E Networks Television. Retrieved March 22, 2015 (http://www.biography.com/people/alan-turing-9512017).

Brown, Gordon. "Gordon Brown: I'm Proud to Say Sorry to a Real War Hero." *Telegraph*, September 10, 2009. Retrieved March 25, 2015 (http://www.telegraph.co.uk/news/politics/gordon-brown/6170112/Gordon-Brown-Im-proud-to-say-sorry-to-a-real-war-hero.html).

"Computer AI Passes Turing Test in 'World First.'" BBC News, June 9, 2014. Retrieved April 5, 2015 (http://www.bbc.com/news/technology-27762088).

Copeland, B. Jack. *Turing: Pioneer of the Information Age*. Oxford, England: Oxford University Press, 2012.

"Decoding History: A World War II Navajo Code Talker in His Own Words." *In America*, December 4, 2011. Retrieved May 17, 2015 (http://inamerica.blogs.cnn.com/2011/12/04/decoding-history-a-world-war-ii-navajo-code-talker-in-his-own-words/).

Eldridge, Jim. *Alan Turing* (Real Lives). London, England: Bloomsbury, 2013.

"The Enigma of Alan Turing." Central Intelligence Agency, April 10, 2015. Retrieved May 19, 2015 (https://www.cia.gov/news-information/ featured-story-archive/2015-featured-story-archive/the-enigma-of-alan-turing.html).

"Family of Alan Turing to Demand Government Pardon 49,000 Other Men." *Guardian*, February 22, 2015. Retrieved May 19, 2015 (http://www. theguardian.com/science/2015/feb/22/ family-alan-turing-government-petition-pardons-gross-indecency-homosexuality).

Fitzsimmons, Emma G. "Alan Turing, Enigma Code-Breaker and Computer Pioneer, Wins Royal Pardon." *New York Times*, December 23, 2013. Retrieved March 25, 2015 (http://www. nytimes.com/2013/12/24/world/europe/alan-turing-enigma-code-breaker-and-computer-pioneer-wins-royal-pardon.html?_r=0).

Harding, Louette. "Life Story: Why Code-breaker Alan Turing Was Cast aside by Postwar Britain."

MailOnline, November 16, 2013. Retrieved May 9, 2015 (http://www.dailymail.co.uk/home/you/article-2507393/Life-story-Why-code-breaker-Alan-Turing-cast-aside-postwar-Britain.html).

Henderson, Harry. *Alan Turing: Computing Genius and Wartime Code Breaker*. New York, NY: Chelsea House, 2011.

Hodges, Andrew. "Alan Turing: A Short Biography." Retrieved March 22, 2015 (http://www.turing.org.uk/bio/).

Hodges, Andrew. *Alan Turing, the Enigma: The Book That Inspired the Film,* The Imitation Game. Princeton, NJ: Princeton University Press, 2014.

Isaacson, Walter. "The Price of Genius." *Time* 184, no. 21/22 (December 2014): 66.

Kirby, Dean. "Sunflower Experiment Proves Alan Turing Was Right." *Manchester Evening News*, October 30, 2012. Retrieved May 18, 2015 (http://www.manchestereveningnews.co.uk/news/greater-manchester-news/sunflower-experiment-proves-alan-turing-801395).

"Labour Backs 'Turing Law' to Quash Historical Gay Convictions." *BBC News*, March 3, 2015.

Retrieved March 25, 2015 (http://www.bbc.com/news/uk-politics-31707197).

Sample, Ian, and Alex Hern. "Scientists Dispute Whether Computer 'Eugene Goostman' Passed Turing Test." *Guardian*, June 9, 2014. Retrieved May 16, 2015 (http://www.theguardian.com/technology/2014/jun/09/scientists-disagree-over-whether-turing-test-has-been-passed).

Swinford, Stephen. "Alan Turing Granted Royal Pardon by the Queen." *Telegraph*, December 24, 2014. Retrieved March 23, 2015 (http://www.telegraph.co.uk/history/world-war-two/10536246/Alan-Turing-granted-Royal-pardon-by-the-Queen.html).

Turing, A. M. "The Chemical Basis of Morphogenesis." *Philosophical Transactions of the Royal Society of London. Series B, Biological Sciences* 59 (1950): 433–460. Retrieved September 11, 2015 (http://www.dna.caltech.edu/courses/cs191/paperscs191/turing.pdf).

Turing, A. M. "Computing Machinery and Intelligence." *Computing Machinery and Intelligence*. Retrieved May 5, 2015 (http://www.abelard.org/turpap/turpap.php#index).

"The Turing Digital Archive." King's College, Cambridge. Retrieved March 22, 2015 (http://turing-archive.org).

"Turing Papers That Cracked Nazi Code Were Used As Draught Excluders." *Times* [London, England] (January 31, 2015): 5.

Turing, Sara. *Alan M. Turing: Centenary Edition.* Cambridge, England: Cambridge University Press, 2012.

Wainwright, Martin. "Grow a Sunflower to Solve Unfinished Alan Turing Experiment." *Guardian*, March 26, 2012. Retrieved September 11, 2015 (http://www.theguardian.com/uk/the-northerner/2012/mar/26/alan-turing-sunflowers-manchester-science-festival).

Index

ABOUT THE AUTHOR

Rebecca Kraft Rector is a former computer network manager and a longtime librarian. She has written science fiction and adventure novels and over one hundred nonfiction articles. She enjoys solving cryptograms, crossword puzzles, and anagrams but is not good enough to have qualified to work as a code breaker at Bletchley Park.

PHOTO CREDITS